Butterfield School
Learning Center
1441 W. Lake Street
Libertyville, IL 60048

DEMCO

P is for Princess

A Royal Alphabet

Written by Steven L. Layne and Deborah Dover Layne
Illustrated by Robert and Lisa Papp

Sleeping Bear Press™

315 E. Eisenhower Pkwy., Suite 200
Ann Arbor, MI 48108
www.sleepingbearpress.com

Sleeping Bear Press is an imprint of Gale, a part of Cengage Learning.

Printed and bound in the United States.

10 9 8 7 6 5 4

Library of Congress Cataloging-in-Publication Data

Layne, Steven L.
P is for princess : a royal alphabet / written by Steven L. Layne and Deborah
Dover Layne ; illustrated by Robert Papp and Lisa Papp.
p. cm.
Summary: "An A through Z picture book introducing royalty from around the
world, both real and make-believe. Topics such as Aurora, emperor, Grace Kelly,
Princess, Ka'iulani, King Arthur, nobility, and tiara are included"
—Provided by publisher.
Includes bibliographical references.
ISBN-13: 978-1-58536-306-3
1. Courts and courtiers—Juvenile literature. 2. Courts and courtiers—Folklore.
3. Fairy tales. 4. Alphabet books. I. Layne, Deborah Dover. II. Papp, Robert. III.
Papp, Lisa. IV. Title.

GT3510.L39 2007
390'.22—dc22   2006026874

Printed by Bang Printing, Brainerd, MN, 4ᵗʰ Ptg., 03/2011

A royal alphabet—what fun!
There's lots to learn before you're done.
Some tales are true; some make-believe.
We'll tell you some before you leave.

Come study princesses and kings,
crown jewels and more majestic things.
The reading's going to be your part.
So turn the page . . . and you can start!

A a

Sleeping Beauty is a classic fairy tale. It is the first in the set of *"Mother Goose Tales"* published by Charles Perrault in 1697. Sleeping Beauty is named for the story of a wicked queen who causes a beautiful princess to prick her finger on the needle of a spinning wheel and to fall into a deep sleep. For 100 years a spell is cast over the entire kingdom, and the princess and her kingdom sleep until she is awakened by the love of her handsome prince.

The name Princess Aurora first appears in Tchaikovsky's 1890 ballet entitled *Sleeping Beauty* which debuted in St. Petersburg, Russia. This ballet was based on both Perrault's original tale and the Brothers Grimm 1812 version of his work Little Brier-Rose. In 1959 Walt Disney released an animated film version of Sleeping Beauty.

A is for Aurora,
a princess put to sleep.
Awakened by a prince's kiss,
she fell in love so deep.

A grand event for royalty
provides us with our letter **B**.
It's sure to be enjoyed by all.
This formal dance is called a Ball.

A *ball* is a lavish and formal party featuring social dancing. The word "ball" comes from the Latin word *ballare* which means "to dance." Historically, those who attend a ball wear formal or fancy clothing. Women typically wear full-length ball gowns and men wear suits or tuxedoes. The magical tale of *Cinderella* illustrates this point when a fairy godmother transforms a simple maiden into a beautifully clothed and elegant lady so that she might attend the royal ball.

The popular phrase *belle of the ball* originally referred to the most beautiful or best-dressed woman at a ball or dance. In French, the word *belle* means beautiful woman, and the word came to be used in English in the early seventeenth century. While this phrase is still used today, its meaning has changed slightly. No longer does the phrase refer to a woman at a ball, but instead it describes the loveliest woman at any social gathering or function.

B b

Legend's most sought-after prince
was quite a handsome fella.
The **C** who won him, lost her shoe—
of course, she's Cinderella.

Cinderella is considered the most famous and popular of all fairy tales. There are literally hundreds of versions of this classic tale. Scholars believe the earliest rendering of the story originated in China around A. D. 860. The best-known version was written by French author Charles Perrault in 1697.

The familiar plot revolves around a young girl whose cruel stepmother and stepsisters treat her like a servant in her own home. Cinderella accepts the help of her "fairy godmother" who transforms her in time to attend a royal ball and gain the attention of the handsome prince.

Walt Disney made the story of Cinderella his twelfth animated feature film, and it was chosen for its similarity to *Snow White and the Seven Dwarfs*, which was a big success for the Disney studios. *Cinderella* was released to theaters in 1950.

The story of *Cinderella* is timeless and has formed the basis of many different kinds of works. Her story has been told through opera, ballet, pantomime, musical comedy, film, and book format.

Dd

Diana has to be our **D**.
A princess known for charity,
her memory burns long and bright—
a candle in the darkest night.

Diana Frances Spencer was born on July 1, 1961, and was the youngest daughter of Edward Spencer. In 1975 Edward became the 8th Earl Spencer, and she was given the title the Lady Diana Spencer.

The Spencers had been close to the British royal family for decades. Diana's maternal grandmother, Lady Fermoy, was a lady-in-waiting to Queen Elizabeth, the Queen Mother. Her father also spent most of his life in royal service to both King George VI and his daughter Queen Elizabeth II. On July 29, 1981, before 3,500 invited guests and a worldwide television audience, Diana married Prince Charles. On that day she became *Her Royal Highness the Princess of Wales* and was ranked the third most senior royal woman in the United Kingdom.

The Princess gave birth to two sons, William and Harry, and became well known for her charity work with AIDS issues and for her international campaign against land mines. During her lifetime she was the most photographed and famous woman in the world, affectionately referred to as "Princess Di." She died in 1997 in an automobile accident near Paris. Many still refer to her as "The People's Princess."

E e

The first Emperor of China,
our E—Qin Shi Huangdi
started building a great wall
that left a mark on history.

An emperor is the ruler of an empire which is a group of nations or states. In contrast, a king rules only one area or people. Since 1800, emperors have ruled China, France, Germany, Japan, and Russia at one time or another. The wife of an emperor or a woman who rules an empire is called an *empress*.

Qin Shi Huangdi (Ch'in Shih-huang-ti) was the first emperor of China. When he was just thirteen years old he became king of the powerful Chinese state of Qin in 247 B.C. At this time in history China was divided into many states or kingdoms. Through a series of wars, the young king unified China's independent states to create a single empire in 221 B.C. and become its first emperor.

Emperor Huangdi accomplished a number of amazing tasks during his reign. First, he organized a single government to run the large empire. Next, he standardized ancient China's laws, money, roads, weights and measures, and written language. This was significant because each of the states that existed independently had a different system. He also mobilized hundreds of thousands of men and ordered the construction of an enormous defensive wall which linked several already existing walls. This was the emperor's way of protecting the northern border and was the precursor to the Great Wall of China.

Qin Shi Huangdi was probably best known for the army of clay, known as the terra-cotta army which was discovered in pits surrounding his burial site. Chinese historical records indicate that over 700,000 men from all parts of the empire worked to build this burial site, taking approximately 38 years to finish. The goal was to build a complete army of warriors and horses in clay to serve the emperor after death. The first pit containing these figures was discovered in 1974. To date, over 7,000 life-sized terra-cotta soldiers and horses as well as bronze horses and chariots have been discovered and are on display in a large museum complex in China.

In Fairy tales we find some magic,
danger, love, and mystery.
To read of mermaids and of giants
letter F can be the key.

A fairy tale usually features interesting characters such as fairies, goblins, mermaids, elves, trolls, giants, dwarfs, and others. These stories often involve royalty, the presence of magic, talking animals, and they usually have a happy ending. Fairy tales were first told orally and then handed down from generation to generation in this format. Some of the most famous writers of fairy tales include Charles Perrault, the Brothers Grimm, Hans Christian Andersen, and Walt Disney.

Charles Perrault was born in Paris, France. Two of his most popular fairy tales are *Sleeping Beauty* and *Cinderella*.

Grimm's Fairy Tales is a famous collection of German folk tales that were collected by two brothers, Jacob and Wilhelm Grimm.

Hans Christian Andersen was Denmark's most famous author, known as the Prince of Storytellers. His fairy tales are among the most widely read works in all of children's literature. Creating 156 tales in all, scholars agree he wrote with wisdom, simplicity, and sly humor.

Walt Disney was born in 1901 in Chicago, Illinois, and is most well known for being a successful storyteller and American film producer. He and his brother Roy began the Disney Brothers studios and later renamed them the Walt Disney Studios. Walt enjoyed a successful 43-year Hollywood career.

Ff

G g

Prince Rainier made her his bride.
Grace Kelly is our **G**.
Her work in film was recognized
by the Academy.

Grace Patricia Kelly was born in Philadelphia and was the third of four children born to Jack and Margaret Kelly. The Kellys were prominent figures in Philadelphia society.

Before beginning her film career, Grace became a fashion model and television actress. She made her motion-picture debut in 1951 in the movie *Fourteen Hours*. In 1955 she won the Academy Award, also known as the Oscar, as best actress for her performance as Georgie Elgin in the movie *The Country Girl*. Grace made a total of eleven movies and was at the height of fame when she decided to retire from her career as an actress and leave Hollywood for what would become the role of a lifetime.

In April of 1956, after months of secret letter writing and a whirlwind romance, Grace Kelly married Prince Rainier III of Monaco. Her Serene Highness, Princess Grace brought glamour and respect to Monaco which is located in the south of France. She and the prince had three children—Princess Caroline, Prince Albert, and Princess Stephanie. In September of 1982 Princess Grace suffered a stroke while driving her car near Monaco. She died the next day without ever regaining consciousness.

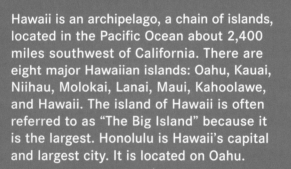

Hawaii is an archipelago, a chain of islands, located in the Pacific Ocean about 2,400 miles southwest of California. There are eight major Hawaiian islands: Oahu, Kauai, Niihau, Molokai, Lanai, Maui, Kahoolawe, and Hawaii. The island of Hawaii is often referred to as "The Big Island" because it is the largest. Honolulu is Hawaii's capital and largest city. It is located on Oahu.

Hawaii's first people were Polynesians. In the 1700s several chiefs ruled the island. Hawaii was united under a single ruler for the first time by 1810. It became known as the Kingdom of Hawaii under the rule of King Kamahameha I.

Victoria Ka'iulani (kah-ee-oo-LAH-nee) was born on October 16, 1875, to Princess Miriam Likelike and her wealthy husband Archibald Cleghorn. Princess Likelike was the sister of King Kalakaua. Since the king had no children of his own, Princess Ka'iulani became an heir to the throne. All of Hawaii rejoiced at her birth. The name Ka'iulani means "the royal sacred one."

A part of island history
is Princess Ka'iulani.
Our H—the state—Hawaii.
She lived in such a lovely place
—the state—Hawaii.

In the 1880s Princess Ka'iulani was in school in England. She received news that a powerful group of mostly American men known as "the haoles" wanted to annex Hawaii to the United States which meant that America would completely take over her country. On January 16, 1893, a company of American marines marched into Honolulu and successfully forced Queen Lili'uokalani to give up her throne.

Princess Ka'iulani traveled to the United States to meet with President Grover Cleveland who agreed to block the annexation as long as he was president. After President Cleveland left office, Congress voted to annex Hawaii. On August 12, 1898, the formal Annexation Day arrived, and the Hawaiian flag no longer flew. A few months later the last Hawaiian Princess, Ka'iulani, died at the young age of 23, and all of Hawaii mourned her death.

This **I**
A queen from Spain is owed our thanks.
is Isabella.
She sent a famous sailor out—
Columbus was the fella.

Isabella I was the queen of the Spanish kingdom of Castille. She married Ferdinand II of Aragon in 1469. The marriage led to the union of Spain's two largest kingdoms. Isabella and her husband were largely responsible for unifying Spain into one of Europe's most powerful nations.

One of Queen Isabella's greatest accomplishments was her decision to provide financial support for Christopher Columbus and to share his vision of sailing westward to the Indies. For five years Columbus tried to convince the queen to sponsor his dream and exploration. In 1492 Columbus finally made that dream a reality with the help of Isabella. Although he did not find the Indies during this voyage, Columbus did make his way to North America. Opening up the New World to settlement and exploration brought enormous financial gain to Queen Isabella and to Spain.

I i

J stands for Jordan,
   home of beloved queens,
among them Noor and Rania,
   who both have reigned supreme.

J j

The country of Jordan is located in the Middle East. It shares its borders with the countries of Syria, Saudi Arabia, Iraq, and Israel. Citizens of Jordan are known as Jordanians.

Her Majesty Queen Noor was born Lisa Najeeb Halaby in Washington, D.C. She married King Hussein in 1978 and became Queen Noor. As queen, she has worked tirelessly to help bridge the gap between western and Middle Eastern cultures and to strengthen the country of Jordan.

Rania Al-Yassin was born in Kuwait, and in 1990 her family moved to Jordan. She married Prince Abdullah on June 10, 1993. Upon the death of King Hussein in 1999, Abdullah and Rania became King and Queen of Jordan. At that time Rania was just 29 years old, making her the world's youngest living queen. Queen Rania has become famous for her efforts to improve educational opportunities for girls and the rights of women.

King Arthur was a legendary king of medieval Britain who became the central figure in some of the most popular stories in all of literature. For over 1,000 years the legends of Arthur's bravery and adventures with his Knights of the Round Table have been passed down from one generation to the next. Historians believe that a real King Arthur probably existed, but no one will ever know for certain who he was or when he lived. Storytellers first began telling the tales of King Arthur by word of mouth. The first written stories began to appear around the year 1135.

According to legend, Arthur was often aided by Merlin the Magician. With Merlin's help, Arthur acquired the magic sword known as Excalibur. King Arthur's favorite residence was Camelot, a castle in southern England where he married Lady Guinevere. As a wedding gift, Guinevere's father, King Leodegrance, brought a magnificent round table built to seat King Arthur's chosen knights. The final seat at the table was reserved for the truest of all knights, Sir Lancelot.

K k

King Arthur's legends and his Knights provide a double K. The famous tales involving them will never fade away.

Ladies-in-waiting—what do they do?
Besides provide our L?
Their duties are quite varied
and the royals think they're swell.

L
l

A lady-in-waiting is a personal assistant who attends to the needs of a queen, princess, or other noblewoman; she is not considered a servant. A lady-in-waiting is often a noblewoman herself although she usually has a lower rank than the one she is assisting. Her duties often vary from monarchy to monarchy, but she commonly serves as a royal companion and accompanies the queen or princess wherever she goes. Today, in the royal household of the United Kingdom, the senior lady-in-waiting is called the Mistress of the Robes.

In Tudor England, ladies-in-waiting were divided into four categories whose titles included great ladies, ladies of the privy chamber, maids of honour, and chamberers. The ladies of the privy chamber were the ones closest to the queen. Most others were maids of honour. Female relatives were often appointed because it was believed they could be trusted.

Those who enter royal service tend to regard it as a lifelong commitment. One characteristic needed for this role is the ability to keep things that are said and done private.

A Monarch is a ruler.
We'll say the **M** in charge.
And several countries have them
from very small to rather large.

Monarchies have existed in all periods of history and in almost every part of the world. A monarchy is a form of government in which one person, the monarch, either inherits or is elected to a throne and is head of state for life. These monarchs have different titles which can include king or queen, emperor, or sultan.

Originally, the power of the monarch was unlimited. At that time, many believed the ruler was only responsible to God. This view began to change during the 1790s when limited or constitutional monarchies developed, and the monarch's duties became mostly ceremonial and symbolic. Today, in modern constitutional monarchies, the executive power is usually carried out by a prime minister and cabinet rather than the monarch. Examples of countries that currently have constitutional monarchies include Denmark, Japan, Norway, Sweden, and the United Kingdom. Currently, there are fewer monarchies than at any time in history.

Nobility is a group or class of people who are considered to be some of the most important in their society. They are said to stand at the top of the social ladder. Nobility is inherited and carries titles such as *duke* or *viscount*. Some nobles have also inherited land as well as their titles.

The British nobility is called *peerage*, and noblemen are known as *peers*. There are five grades of peers. Ranking from highest to lowest they include duke, marquess or marquis, earl, viscount, and baron. Duke is the highest hereditary rank below that of prince. Earl is equal in rank to a continental count. Women who hold these titles on their own or are wives of these noblemen are identified as peeresses. The five grades of peeresses include duchess, marchioness, countess, viscountess, and baroness.

N n

N begins Nobility,
and peerage is their order.
It classifies them for succession
inside Britain's border.

Oo

The Ruler's Orb is a hollow, golden globe which was created for the coronation ceremony of King Charles II in 1661. It is one of the British crown jewels. Coronation is a ceremony at which a king or queen publicly receives a crown as a symbol of his or her authority and promises to rule wisely.

During the ceremony, the Coronation Ring is placed on the ruler's right hand. This symbolizes the marriage between the ruler and the kingdom. The ruler is also given two scepters. At the top of one scepter is the *Star of Africa* which is the largest cut diamond in the world. At the same time the ruler is holding both scepters, he or she is crowned with St. Edward's Crown.

The term crown jewels refers to the objects a ruler uses or wears during the coronation ceremony and other important gatherings. Some items that make up the *crown jewels* include crowns, scepters, swords, orbs, rings, the royal robe, and several other objects.

Letter O is for an orb.
It's one of the crown jewels.
A holy cross adorns the top—
it's part of coronation's tools.

Princess is the feminine form of prince which comes from the Latin word *princeps* which means "principle citizen." A princess attains her title by being the daughter of a king or the wife of a prince. A prince and/or princess is usually the hereditary ruler of a country.

Pocahontas was born around 1595 in what is now Virginia. She was the daughter of Powhatan, chief of the Powhatan people. Historians believe that Pocahontas was between ten and twelve years old when she first encountered the colonists who had sailed from England and landed in Jamestown, Virginia. Pocahontas visited Jamestown often and became friends with its leader, John Smith. She worked to keep peace between the colonists and her people. John Smith even claims that Pocahontas helped save his life.

In 1614 Pocahontas married John Rolfe in England and took the name Rebecca Rolfe. Pocahontas spent many years of her life helping the English, the colonists, and her own Indian people learn about each other and understand each other's way of life. The English thought of her as an Indian "princess." At the age of 22, Pocahontas died of smallpox and was buried in England. Today, a statue of Pocahontas in Jamestown and the "Princess Pocahontas Gardens" in Gravesend, England, honor her important contributions to both countries' histories.

Pp

P is for Princess.
For many girls a dream
to marry a tall handsome prince
and make the royal scene.

Pocahontas is a P
who also deserves mention.
She bridged two cultures' differences
with truly good intentions.

Elizabeth the II is
a queen who's quite well known.
She's reigned for over fifty years;
this **Q** calls England home.

Q

Queen is the title of a woman who rules a kingdom in her own right or who is the wife of a king. Elizabeth II is the queen of the United Kingdom and Northern Ireland. She became queen in 1952 after the death of her father, King George VI. After the official year of mourning for the previous monarch, her coronation ceremony took place. The queen's primary public role is to attend ceremonial state occasions and to represent the United Kingdom as she visits countries throughout the world.

In November of 1947, Elizabeth married Philip Mountbatten. Philip was a British naval lieutenant and a member of the Greek royal family. He became Prince Philip, Duke of Edinburgh. The queen and Prince Philip have four children. Charles, Prince of Wales is the oldest son and heir to the throne. Their other children include Anne, Princess Royal, Andrew, Duke of York, and Prince Edward, Earl of Wessex.

In 2002 Queen Elizabeth II celebrated her Golden Jubilee, marking the 50th anniversary of her accession to the throne. Currently, at the age of 80, she remains a highly-respected head of state.

Once upon a time rolling out the red carpet was reserved for kings and queens. In the United States, the phrase *roll out the red carpet* dates back to the early 1900s. When important guests would visit a hotel, for example, or other public place, a special red carpet was traditionally unrolled at the building's entrance to welcome them with great hospitality or ceremony. Some people believe this act itself was how the phrase gained its popularity. Others believe it has a more specific source. That source was the red carpet that led passengers to the Twentieth Century Limited, the best-known train in the United States which made its debut in 1902. This train ran between New York and Chicago and consisted of all first-class accommodations. People riding on this train were considered to be receiving *the red-carpet treatment*, which means living in the height of luxury.

Today, one place the red carpet is frequently found is in Hollywood, California. Many famous television and movie actors and actresses are commonly referred to as *Hollywood Royalty*. Several of the awards programs that honor the very best in film and television have a long red carpet leading up to the buildings in which they are held. Some examples of these awards ceremonies include the Golden Globe Awards, the Emmy Awards, and the Academy Awards (also known as the Oscars). The stars famously walk the red carpet before these ceremonies, pausing to be photographed and admired by their fans.

R is for Red carpet
that signifies a star,
both royal-born and Hollywood
with fans both near and far.

Snow White is the main character of a well-known fairy tale. Many retellings of this popular tale exist, but perhaps the most famous version was written by Jacob and Wilhelm Grimm (the Brothers Grimm) and first published in 1812. The origin of this tale is unknown, but scholars believe it originated somewhere in Asia and is likely no older than the Middle Ages.

In the story, a queen gives birth to a baby girl who has skin as white as snow, lips as red as blood, and hair as black as ebony. They name her Princess Snow White. When the queen dies, the king takes another wife who is jealous of Snow White's beauty. This puts her in danger. Snow White hides in the forest with seven little men, the dwarfs, and they take care of each other. The queen discovers Snow White and puts her to sleep until the prince arrives to rescue her.

In 1937 Walt Disney released his first full-length, animated feature film entitled *Snow White and the Seven Dwarfs*. The movie was adapted from the Brothers Grimm fairy tale.

S Living with the seven dwarfs
our S must be Snow White.
Prince Charming saved her—and turns out
that he was "Mr. Right."

Tiaras make a classy T.
They first were worn by royalty.
We see them still in formal dress
when famous ladies look their best.

A tiara is a type of crown. It is a formal headdress made of precious metal and set with beautiful stones or jewels. The tiara has a semicircular band and is kept in place by its wire mount. In ancient times the tiara was worn by kings and emperors and was made of fabric or leather which contained intricate and elaborate decoration. In modern times the tiara is worn by women as part of their attire and not as a symbol of rank. While queens and princesses do wear tiaras to formal functions, they are also worn by women who are not of royal heritage. For example, tiaras are frequently used to "crown" beauty pageant winners. They are also worn at times by the bride as part of a wedding outfit.

It is believed that Queen Elizabeth II has the largest and most valuable collection of tiaras in the world. According to historians, she has received many of them through inheritance and as gifts from foreign countries. Pictures of her tiaras can be found in the book *The Queen's Jewels: The Personal Collection of Elizabeth II* by Leslie Field.

T t

U u

King Ulysses is our **U**.
His grand adventure brought him to
rule Ithaca both day and night
with wisdom and a hero's might.

Ulysses was the king of Ithaca and a brave and shrewd hero in Greek mythology. Mythology is a set of stories, traditions, or beliefs that have developed around one particular person or event. His name occurs in both Greek, as Odysseus, and in Latin as Ulysses. Many of the stories about Ulysses describe his life during and after the Trojan War which was a conflict between Greece and the city of Troy.

Ulysses is a major character in the *Iliad*, and he is the hero of the *Odyssey*. These are two famous epic stories written by the Greek poet known as Homer.

Victoria was crowned queen at Westminster Abbey on June 28, 1838. She was only 18 years old. She ruled as queen of Great Britain and Ireland from 1837 to 1901. Victoria began her reign immediately after the death of the previous ruler, but the formal coronation ceremony did not take place until the official "year of mourning" period had ended. Her sixty-three-year reign has been the longest in British history.

Many important events happened during Victoria's reign. During the first few decades, Britain experienced rapid growth in industry, a large increase in the population, the rise of the British middle class, and a great deal of material prosperity. Her years as queen have become known as the Victorian Age.

Queen Victoria was a wise and capable ruler who was concerned with the welfare of her people. Victoria married Prince Albert in February of 1840, and together they had nine children. In the last decades of her life and reign she received the nickname "Grandmother of Europe." The nickname is accurate because many of her children and grandchildren have married into some of Europe's royal families including those in Spain, Russia, Sweden, Norway, and Romania.

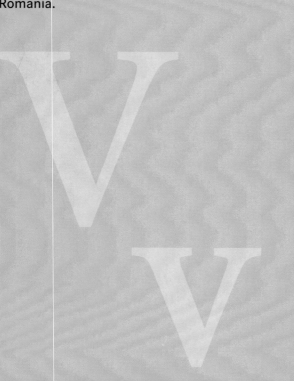

Victoria—a famous queen
from English history.
Became a ruler at eighteen
and she's our letter V.

W

A castle makes a splendid home
for real-life royals and those in tales.
Our **W**'s a famous one—
it's Windsor found southeast of Wales.

Windsor Castle is located in the town of Windsor near London, England. It is one of three official residences of Her Majesty, Queen Elizabeth II and is the largest inhabited castle in the world. It is also the oldest royal residence, having been continually occupied by ruling monarchs of Britain for approximately 900 years. Over the years, different rulers have added on to the castle. Today it covers over nine acres. One of the most striking features of the castle is the round tower which was completed in 1528. The tower stands about 100 feet high.

In 1993 the castle experienced a severe fire, and over 100 rooms were damaged or destroyed. It took more than 200 firefighters 15 hours and 1.5 million gallons of water to put it out. Restoration of the castle cost millions of dollars and took five years to complete. Today sections of the castle are open to the public and tours may be taken most days of the year.

Xerxes was a clever king
who built a famous bridge of boats.
This Persian ruler is our X.
His cunning earns him many votes.

King Xerxes I ruled the Persian Empire from 486 B.C. until his death in 465 B.C. Xerxes was the son of King Darius I, and he spent several years trying to achieve his father's goal of conquering Greece. During the early years of his reign, he crushed any challenges to his authority by putting down rebellions in the Persian provinces of Egypt and Babylonia.

A formidable military leader, King Xerxes was patient and thorough in his preparations for war. Proof of this was demonstrated by the ongoing military buildup for the planned invasion of Greece. Long before the army's arrival, engineers and laborers built impressive boat bridges over the Hellespont so the army would be able to cross over the water into Europe. A total of 674 boats were used. Special heavy anchors and cables made from flax and papyrus were used to hold the boats in place. Finally, wooden planks were placed on top of the boats, and a fence was put up on both sides.

King Xerxes had assembled an army and navy that was probably the largest force ever gathered by any ruler up to that time. It took seven days for the Persian army to cross the wooden bridges that Xerxes had built from the boats. His fleet won a victory at Artemisium. His army destroyed the small Spartan army at the Pass of Thermopylae, and Xerxes took the deserted city of Athens and set fire to it.

Xx

Y is for the Duke of York
who's found in nursery rhymes and tales.
The second son of English kings—
he's brother to the Prince of Wales.

Y y

You may remember...

The grand old Duke of York,
He had ten thousand men.
He marched them up to the top of the hill,
And he marched them down again.
When they were up, they were up,
And when they were down, they were down,
And when they were only halfway up,
They were neither up nor down.

York is a city in England. The Duke of York is a title given to the second son of any ruling monarch in Britain. In theory, any second son of a monarch who led an army could be the subject of this rhyme. Scholars disagree as to whom this famous verse actually refers. Some say it refers to Frederick, Duke of York, in his battle with Napoleon. Others believe it refers to the defeat of Richard, Duke of York, in the War of the Roses in 1455. This was a war between the House of York, whose symbol was a white rose, and the House of Lancaster, whose symbol was a red rose. The war lasted for over 30 years and could be considered a civil war.

The term *czar* (also spelled *tsar* and pronounced *zar*) comes from the Latin word *Caesar* which means emperor. During the fifteenth century, Russia's Prince Ivan III began using the term *czar* to introduce an added level of power and majesty to his rule. On January 16, 1547, his sixteen-year-old son, Prince Ivan IV, was the first to be crowned czar of all Russia.

Czar was used as the title for a male monarch in Russia. His wife's title was *czarina*. When Russia crowned a female monarch, she was given the title *czaritsa*. The last czar was Nicholas II. The title *czar* was used until 1721 when Peter the Great began westernizing Russia. He changed the title from czar to emperor. In modern times, the government of the Russian Federation is run by an elected president.

The sound your ears first hear is Z
when you say cZar (with silent "c").
These rulers come from Russia's past.
The royal title didn't last.

The reign of our royal alphabet
has now come to an end.
We hope you'll open up this book
and read from it again.

Royal Facts

1. Where is Windsor Castle located?

2. Who was the explorer Queen Isabella helped to send on a famous voyage?

3. Who is known as the Prince of Storytellers?

4. Name any two items that are a part of the British crown jewels.

5. Name the form of government in which one person either inherits or is elected to the throne.

6. Who is believed to own the most valuable collection of tiaras in the world?

7. What do people who attend a "ball" typically wear?

8. Name two famous writers of fairy tales.

9. What is an empire and who rules it?

10. Name the five grades of peers in order from highest to lowest.

11. Who was well known for her charity work?

12. What is the special title given to the senior lady-in-waiting?

13. Who ordered a bridge to be built out of boats?

14. What did Grace Kelly win in 1955?

15. Name a brave hero from Greek mythology. By what other name is he known?

16. Who is known as "The Grandmother of Europe?"

17. In the year 2002, what did Queen Elizabeth celebrate?

18. What was discovered in the pits surrounding Emperor Qin Shi Huangdi's burial site?

Answers

1. in the city of Windsor, near London
2. Christopher Columbus
3. Hans Christian Andersen
4. crowns, scepters, swords, orbs, rings, or the royal robe
5. a monarchy
6. Queen Elizabeth II
7. formal or fancy clothing; a ball gown, suit, or tuxedo
8. Charles Perrault, Hans Christian Andersen, Jacob Grimm, Wilhelm Grimm, or Walt Disney
9. a group of nations or states — an emperor
10. Duke, Marquess or Marquis, Earl, Viscount, Baron
11. Diana, Princess of Wales
12. Mistress of the Robes
13. King Xerxes I
14. The Academy Award or The Oscar
15. King Ulysses — Odysseus
16. Queen Victoria
17. Her Golden Jubilee or 50 years as monarch or ruler
18. The terra-cotta army or an army made of clay

Steven Layne

Steven Layne serves as a full-time faculty member in the Department of Education at Judson University in Elgin, Illinois, where he teaches courses in reading methods as well as in children's and adolescent literature.

A respected literacy consultant, motivational keynote speaker, and featured author, Dr. Layne works with large numbers of educators and children during school visits and at conferences held throughout the world each year. His work has been recognized with awards for outstanding contributions to the fields of educational research, teaching, and writing. For more information visit www.stevelayne.com.

Deborah Dover Layne

Over the course of 20 years in the field of education Deborah Layne has worked at both the elementary and middle school levels and has been a reading specialist. She has also served as a professor of reading at the graduate and undergraduate levels and supervised pre-service teachers in addition to her role as wife and mother of four.

Robert Papp

Robert Papp says he is one fortunate guy. Every day he gets up and plays with paint! Drawing and painting since a boy, Robert was formally trained at duCret School of Art in New Jersey, where he learned how to create memorable art. His paintings have won awards and garnered attention nationwide, but he is most proud of the reaction he gets from the children who view his work, and who always seem to notice each and every brushstroke.

Lisa Papp

Lisa Papp attended Iowa State University College of Design for one year, and studied three more years at duCret School of Art in New Jersey where she won numerous awards for her watercolor paintings. She also illustrated *One for All: A Pennsylvania Alphabet* for Sleeping Bear Press. Lisa says, "I am lucky to illustrate. It gives me a chance to dream and see it come to life." She currently resides in historic Bucks County, Pennsylvania with her artist husband, Rob, and their whimsical cat, Taffy.

Bibliography

Arnstein, W. L. (2003). Queen Victoria. New York: Palgrave Macmillan.

Barnhart, R. K. (1988). The Barnhart Dictionary of Etymology. Bronx, NY: The H. W. Wilson Company.

Best of Britain's Castles: One Hundred of the Most Impressive Historic Sites in Britain. (2004). Windsor: A A Publishing.

Bramwell, N. D. (2004). Ancient Persia. Berkeley Heights, NJ: Enslow Publishers, Inc.

British Broadcasting Corporation. (1992, November 20). Blaze Rages in Windsor Castle. Retrieved July 25, 2006 from the World Wide Web: http://news.bbc.co.uk/onthisday/hi/ dates/stories/november/20/newsid_2551000/2551107.stm

British Broadcasting Corporation. (1997, November 17). Windsor Castle: Five Years from Disaster to Triumph. Retrieved July 25, 2006 from the World Wide Web: http://news.bbc.co.uk/1/hi/ special_report/31069.stm

Chiflet, J. L., and Beaulet, A. (1996). Victoria and Her Times. New York: Henry Holt and Company, Inc.

Claiborne, R. (1988). Loose Cannons and Red Herrings: A Book of Lost Metaphors. New York: W. W. Norton and Company.

Claybourne, A. (1998). Greek Mythology: Ulysses and the Trojan War. London: Usborne Publishing.

Clayton, T., and Craig, P. (2001). Diana: Story of a Princess. New York: Simon & Schuster, Inc.

Cole, M. D. (1996). Walt Disney: Creator of Mickey Mouse. Berkeley Heights, NJ: Enslow Publishers, Inc.

Cotterell, A. (1981). The First Emperor of China. New York: Holt, Rinehart and Winston.

Edens, C. (2004). Princess Stories. San Francisco: Chronicle Books LLC.

Field, L. (1987). The Queen's Jewels: The Personal Collection of Elizabeth II. New York: Harry N. Abrams, Inc.

Ford, C. T. (2003). Walt Disney: Meet the Cartoonist. Berkeley Heights, NJ: Enslow Publishers, Inc.

Goldberg, J. (1998). Celebrate the States: Hawaii. New York: Benchmark Books.

Goode, D. (1988). Cinderella. New York: Random House, Inc.

Graham, T. (2002). Queen Elizabeth II: A Celebration of Her Majesty's Fifty-Year Reign. New York: Rizzoli International Publications, Inc.

Greene, C. (1991). Hans Christian Andersen: Prince of Storytellers. Chicago: Childrens Press.

Hettinga, D. R. (2001). The Brothers Grimm: Two Lives, One Legacy. New York: Clarion Books.

Hoey, B. (1991). Charles & Diana: The 10th Anniversary. New York: Penguin Books USA, Inc.

Holberg, A. (1994). Forms of Address: A Guide for Business and Social Use. Houston: Rice University Press.

Hudson's Historic Houses and Gardens, Castles, and Heritage Sites: The Comprehensive Annual Guide to Heritage Properties in Great Britain and Northern Ireland. (2005). Guilford, CT: The Globe Pequot Press.

Hyman, T. S. (1977). The Sleeping Beauty. New York: Little, Brown and Company.

Hyman, T. S. (1974). Snow White. New York: Little, Brown and Company.

Kent, D. (2004). Hawaii's Road to Statehood. New York: Children's Press.

Kipfer, B.A. (1997). The Order of Things: How Everything in the World is Organized…into Hierarchies, Structures, & Pecking Orders. New York: Random House, Inc.

Kirkpatrick, B. (1997). Cliches. New York: St. Martin's Press.

Kummer, P. K. (1998). Hawaii. Mankato, MN: Capstone Press.

Lacey, R. (1994). Grace. Thorndike, ME: G. K. Hall & Company.

Langley, A. (1997). Hans Christian Andersen: The Dreamer of Fairy Tales. New York: Oxford University Press.

Metz, H. C. (1991). Jordan: A Country Study. Washington, DC: Library of Congress.

Middleton, J. (2005). World Monarchies and Dynasties. Armonk, NY: M. E. Sharpe, Inc.

Millar, J. R. (2004). The Encyclopedia of Russian History. New York: Macmillan Reference USA.

Mosley, L. (1990). Disney's World. Lanham, MD: Scarborough House.

Nardo, D. (1998). World History Series: The Persian Empire. San Diego: Lucent Books.

Nardo, D. (1999). Women Leaders of Nations. San Diego: Lucent Books.

Nettleton, P. H. (2004). Pocahontas: Peacemaker and Friend to the Colonists. Minneapolis: Picture Window Books.

Queen Noor. (2003). Leap of Faith: Memoirs of an Unexpected Life. New York: Miramax Books.

Opie, I., and Opie, P. (1988). The Oxford Dictionary of Nursery Rhymes. New York: Oxford University Press.

Philip, N. (1997). Fairy Tales of the Brothers Grimm. New York: Penguin Books USA, Inc.

Philip, N. (2004). Fairy Tales of Hans Christian Andersen. New York: The Reader's Digest Association Limited.

Raatma, L. (2006). Queen Noor: American-Born Queen of Jordan. Minneapolis: Compass Point Books.

Rakieten, E. (Executive Producer). (2006, May 17). The Oprah Winfrey Show [The World's Youngest Queen: An Interview with Queen Rania of Jordan] [Television Broadcast] Chicago: American Broadcasting Company.

Riordan, J. (1998). King Arthur. New York: Oxford University Press.

Roberts, C. (2005). Heavy Words Lightly Thrown: The Reason Behind the Rhyme. New York: Gotham Books.

Ross, S. (2004). Monarchs. New York: Thomson-Gale.

Scholastic. (December 2004). The Grand Old Duke of York. Scholastic. Retrieved July 31, 2006 from the World Wide Web:http://www.scholastic.co.uk/magazines/downloads/a1b5-nel2.pdf

Shaughnessy, D. (1997). Pocahontas: Powhatan Princess. New York: The Rosen Publishing Group.

Shawcross, W. (2002). Queen and Country: The Fifty-Year Reign of Elizabeth II. New York: Simon & Schuster.

Somerset, A. (1984). Ladies-in-Waiting: From the Tudors to the Present Day. New York: Alfred A. Knopf, Inc.

Stanley, F. (1991). The Last Princess: The Story of Princess Ka'iulani of Hawaii. New York: Four Winds Press.

Sterne, E. G., and Lindsay, B. (2002). King Arthur and the Knights of the Round Table. New York: Random House.

Stevens, P. (1988). Ferdinand and Isabella. New York: Chelsea House Publishers.

Wagner, H. L. (2005). King Abdullah II. Philadelphia: Chelsea House Publishers.

Wenli, Z. (1996). The Qin Terracotta Army. London: Scala Books.

Wilkes, A. (1981). The Adventures of King Arthur. Tulsa: Hayes Books.

Williams, M. (1996). King Arthur and the Knights of the Round Table. Cambridge, MA: Candlewick Press.

Wood, S. B. (2002). Queen Elizabeth II: Monarch of Our Times. New York: Raintree Steck-Vaughn Publishers.

The World Book Encyclopedia. (2006). Chicago: World Book, Inc.

Zipes, J. (2000). The Oxford Companion to Fairy Tales. New York: Oxford University Press.

Acknowledgment of Research Assistance

Mary Haley, History Teacher/Historian Butler Junior High School — Oak Brook, Illinois

Michelle Caulk, Research Librarian St. Charles Public Library — St. Charles, Illinois